THE BURNS FEDERATION SONG BOOK

THE BURNS FEDERATION SONG BOOK

Containing twenty songs
of
ROBERT BURNS
arranged for schools

Selected and Edited
for the Burns Federation
by
JOHN McVIE

Musical arrangements
by
GEORGE SHORT

The Burns Federation wish to acknowledge the generous financial assistance of the J. J. Munro Trust in the publication of this book.

PREFACE

This selection of the songs of Robert Burns is intended primarily for use in schools, but should be of interest to all admirers of the poet.

The object of the Burns Federation has been to give an accurate text of the songs, together with a glossary and a phonetic rendering in the Ayrshire dialect of words which, though written in English, should be pronounced in Scots. Notes on pronunciation are given, but if singers prefer to sing the songs with the Scots vowel qualities and intonation of their own district, they should be encouraged to do so.

Many songs of Burns were written to instrumental tunes, with a compass beyond the range of the average child's voice. In a few of the songs, by substituting another note where necessary, the tune has been brought within average range without altering the character of the melody.

Burns's own notes on the songs are given as a matter of interest.

The Burns Federation acknowledges its indebtedness to Mr. George Short for his musical arrangements of the songs and to Mr. David D. Murison, Editor of the *Scottish National Dictionary,* for his notes on pronunciation.

J. M.

NOTES ON PRONUNCIATION

Burns himself spoke the dialect of Ayrshire, but his poetry derives from the general stream of Scottish poetic tradition and his language is modified to suit rhyme and rhythm and the tone and style of each poem. Thus some songs are more Scots than others, No. 16 for instance more than No. 1, which is a medley of Scots and English, while No. 3 is almost entirely in English. In the first verse of No. 8 the repeated *-ng* should be pronounced as in English (not as *-n* in Scots) to preserve the echoing note of the bird's song. Where no marginal transcription has been given, it is understood that the words are to be pronounced according to the English of Scotland.

It should be noted that in Ayrshire, *a* final or before *-n(d)* as in *a', ca', fa', hand, sand, land,* has a rounded sound, as in English *awe,* and that other vowels, except when unstressed, tend to be pronounced long, as in *craidit* (No. 16), *mailoday, roaks* (No. 13), *boanay.* The *d* in *nd* final is dropped, hence *haun,* etc.

Note the following pronunciations where words are unstressed : and (*an*), for (*fur*), has (*hiz*), to (*tay*), was (*wiz*), would (*wid*).

Note also that in Scots, *wh* is pronounced strongly as *hw* as in *hwaw, hwan, hwawr* for who, when, where, and *r* everywhere is trilled.

Some of the pronunciations that Burns would have used are now obsolete, e.g. *thoo* for thou, *jye* for joy, *sall* for shall, *airt* for art (No. 8). *Quo scho* (No. 16) would have been pronounced by him *ko sho* (*ö* as in German). These old pronunciations may be dropped in singing.

The spelling is sometimes Anglicised and obscures the Scots form of the word which should be used, e.g. all for *aw,* who for *hwaw,* of for *o,* how, now for *hoo, noo,* bright for *bricht,* sought for *socht.*

In the phonetic renderings, *ei* is pronounced as *i* in English bite, and *ch* as in High German ich or Nacht, *u* as in but, *zh* as *s* in pleasure.

D. D. M.

CONTENTS

1. Scots wha hae

This lyric was inspired not only by the thought of Bannockburn, but also "by the glowing ideas of some other struggles of the same nature not quite so ancient." (The French Revolution.)

(Letter to Thomson, 1 Sept., 1793)

Scoats	Scots, what hae[1] wi' Wallace bled,	
	Scots, wham[2] Bruce has aften[3] led,	*affen*
	Welcome to your gory bed	
	Or to victorie!	
nooz	Now's the day, and now's the hour:	*oor*
	See the front of battle lour,[4]	*loor*
	See approach proud Edward's power—	*prood, poor*
	Chains and slaverie!	
wull	Wha will be a traitor knave?	
full	Wha can fill a coward's grave?	*coourdz*
	Wha sae base as be a slave?	
	Let him turn, and flee!	
Scoatlunz	Wha for Scotland's King and Law	*Keeng*
	Freedom's sword will strongly draw,	*wull stroanglay*
stawn	Freeman stand or freeman fa',	*faw*
	Let him follow me!	*foala*
	By Oppression's woes and pains,	
	By your sons in servile chains,	
	We will drain our dearest veins	
	But they shall be free!	
prood	Lay the proud usurpers low!	
faw	Tyrants fall in every foe!	
Leeburtay'z	Liberty's in every blow!	
day	Let us do, or die!	*dee*

[1] *who have* [2] *whom* [3] *often* [4] *look threateningly*

1. Scots wha hae

Tune:— Hey, tuttie taitie.

Scotish Airs, 1801, 133.

2. A rosebud by my early walk

"This song I composed on Miss Jenny Cruickshank, only child to my worthy friend Mr. Wm. Cruickshank, of the High School, Edinburgh."

(R. B. in *Interleaved Museum*)

Burns wrote this song to the tune *The Rosebud* composed by David Sillar, but its unvocal intervals make it unfit for performance.

A rose-bud, by my early walk,
Adoon, coarn Adown a corn-inclosed bawk,[1]
Sae gently bent its thorny stalk, *thoarnay stawk*
All on a dewy morning.
Ere twice the shades o' dawn are fled,
aw In a' its crimson glory spread,
And drooping rich the dewy head,
It scents the early morning.

Within the bush, her covert nest
A little linnet fondly prest,
The dew sat chilly on her breast,
Sae early in the morning.
She soon shall see her tender brood,
The pride, the pleasure o' the wood,
Amang the fresh green leaves bedew'd,
Awake the early morning.

So thou, dear bird, young Jeany fair!
On trembling string or vocal air
Shalt sweetly pay the tender care
That tents[2] thy early morning!
So thou, sweet Rose-bud, young and gay,
Shalt beauteous blaze upon the day,
And bless the parent's evening ray
That watch'd thy early morning.

[1] strip left unploughed [2] watches over

2. A rosebud by my early walk

Tune:— The Shepherd's Wife.

Graham's Songs of Scotland III p. 86

3. Afton water

"Written as a compliment to the River Afton which flows into the Nith near New Cumnock, which has some charming wild romantic scenery as its banks."
(Letter to Mrs. Dunlop, 5 Feb., 1789)

Flow gently, sweet Afton, among thy green braes,[1]
Flow gently, I'll sing thee a song in thy praise;
My Mary's asleep by thy murmuring stream,
Flow gently, sweet Afton, disturb not her dream!

Thou stock dove whose echo resounds thro' the glen,
Ye wild whistling blackbirds in yon thorny den,[2]
Thou green-crested lapwing, thy screaming forbear,
I charge you, disturb not my slumbering fair!

How lofty, sweet Afton, thy neighbouring hills,
Far mark'd with the courses of clear, winding rills;
There daily I wander, as noon rises high,
My flocks and my Mary's sweet cot in my eye.

How pleasant thy banks and green vallies below,
Where wild in the woodlands the primroses blow;
There oft, as mild Ev'ning weeps over the lea,
The sweet-scented birk[3] shades my Mary and me.

Thy crystal stream, Afton, how lovely it glides,
And winds by the cot where my Mary resides;
How wanton thy waters her snowy feet lave,
As, gathering sweet flowerets, she stems thy clear wave.

Flow gently sweet Afton, among thy green braes,
Flow gently, sweet river, the theme of my lays;
My Mary's asleep by thy murmuring stream,
Flow gently, sweet Afton, disturb not her dream!

[1] hillsides [2] ravine [3] birch

Afton Water

Tune:— Afton Water.

Scots Musical Museum 1792, No. 386.

4. Ay waukin, o

Stenhouse says that this is a very old fragment altered somewhat by Burns, and to which he prefixed the first verse

The melody is remarkable for its brevity and simplicity.

(Dick's *Songs of Burns,* 1903, p. 402)

Ei Ay waukin,[1] O, *wawkin*
Waukin[2] still and weary;
Sleep I can get nane[3]
thinkin For thinking on my dearie.

Simmer's[4] a pleasant time: *pleezant*
Floorz Flowers of ev'ry colour,
The water rins[5] o'er the heugh,[6] *owr, hyuch*
And I long for my true lover.

When I sleep I dream,
When I wauk[7] I'm eerie,[8]
Sleep I can get nane
For thinking on my dearie.

Lainlay nicht Lanely[9] night comes on,
A' the lave[10] are sleepin
I think on my bonie lad, *boanay lawd*
And I bleer my een wi' greetin[11]

[1] always awake [2] sleepless [3] none [4] summer's [5] runs
[6] crag [7] am sleepless [8] forlorn [9] lonely [10] rest
[11] bedim my eyes with weeping

4. Ay waukin, O

Tune:— Ay waukin, O.

S.M.M. 1790, No. 213.

5. The deil's awa wi' the Exciseman

"Mr. Mitchell mentioned to you a ballad, which I composed and sung at one of his Excise Court dinners — here it is, *The Deil's awa wi' the Exciseman.*"
(Letter to J. Leven, General Supervisor of Excise, Edinburgh, March ?, 1792)

deel The deil[1] cam fiddlin thro' the town, *toon*
awaw And danc'd awa wi' the Exciseman;
And ilka wife[2] cries, — "Auld Mahoun,[3]
I wish you luck o' the prize man!"

Chorus

The deil's awa, the deil's awa,
The deil's awa wi' the Exciseman;
He's danc'd awa, he's danc'd awa,
He's danc'd awa wi' th' Exciseman!

Oor, mawt "We'll mak our maut,[4] and we'll brew our drink,
We'll laugh, sing, and rejoice, man; *rejyze*
munnay And mony braw thanks to the meikle black deil, *meekil*
That danc'd awa wi' th' Exciseman!

"There's threesome[5] reels, there's foursome[6] reels, *fowrsum*
hoarnpeips There's hornpipes and strathspeys, man, *strathspeiz*
yay But the ae[7] best dance e'er cam to the land
Was the deil's awa wi' th' Exciseman!"

[1] Devil [2] every woman [3] old name for the Devil — from Mahomet
[4] malt [5] [6] danced in sets of three or four [7] one

5. The diel's awa wi' the Exciseman

Tune:—The Hemp-dresser

S.M.M. 1792, No. 399

6. Bonie wee thing

"Composed on my little idol, the charming lovely Davies."
(R. B. in *Interleaved Museum*)

Chorus

boanay Bonie[1] wee thing, cannie[2] wee thing, *cawnie*
Lovely wee thing, wert thou mine,
weer I wad wear thee in my bosom,
Lest my jewel I should tine![3]

Wishfully I look and languish
In that bonie face o' thine;
hert And my heart it stounds[4] wi' anguish, *stoonz*
Lest my wee thing be na[5] mine.

Wit and Grace and Love and Beauty,
yay In ae[6] constellation shine;
To adore thee is my duty,
Goddess o' this soul o' mine!

[1] pretty [2] gentle [3] lose [4] throbs [5] not [6] one

6. Bonie wee thing

Tune:—Bonie wee thing. S.M.M. 1792, No. 341.

7. Braw, braw lads on Yarrow braes

"Framed on an older pastoral song of the Borderland and the romantic country of Tweeddale."

(Dick's *Songs of Burns,* 1903, p. 397)

Braw,[1] braw lads on Yarrow braes,
They rove amang the blooming heather;
But Yarrow braes nor Ettrick shaws,[2]
lawdz Can match the lads o' Galla water.

yin But there is ane, a secret ane,
ubin Aboon them a' I lo'e[3] him better; *loo*
un And I'll be his, and he'll be mine,
boanay The bonie lad o' Galla water.

Altho' his daddie was nae laird,[4]
And tho' I hae nae meikle tocher;[5]
Yet, rich in kindest, truest love,
oor floaks We'll tent[6] our flocks by Galla water.

It ne'er was wealth, it ne'er was wealth,
That coft[7] contentment, peace, or pleasure; *pleezhur*
The bands and bliss o' mutual love,
O, that's the chiefest warld's treasure! *treezhur*

[1] *handsome* [2] *woods* [3] *love* [4] *no landowner* [5] *much dowry*
[6] *tend, watch* [7] *bought*

7. Braw, braw, lads on Yarrow Braes

Tune:— Galla Water.

Scotish Airs 1793, I 11.

8. Ca' the yowes to the knowes

(SECOND VERSION)

"I am flattered at your adopting *Ca' the Yowes* as it was owing to me that ever it saw the light."
(Letter to Thomson, Sept., 1794)

(The Clouden is a small tributary of the Nith near Dumfries.)

caw, youz Ca' the yowes to the knowes.[1] *nowz*
hwawr Ca' them where the heather grows, *growz*
Ca, them where the burnie rowes,[2] *rowz*
boanay My bonie dearie.

maivis Hark, the mavis'[3], e'ening sang
Clooden Sounding Clouden's woods amang, *wudz*
Then a-faulding[4] let us gang,[5]
My bonie dearie.

doon We'll gae[6] down by Clouden side,
Thro' the hazels, spreading wide *spreedin*
owr O'er the waves that sweetly glide
tae, min To the moon sae clearly.

Yonder Clouden's silent towers *toorz*
minsheinz Where, at moonshine's midnight hours, *midnicht oor*
owr O'er the dewy bending flowers *bendin floorz*
Fairies dance sae cheery.

Ghaist nor bogle[7] shalt thou fear,
Thou'rt to Love and Heav'n sae dear, *heev'n*
noacht, ull Nocht[8] of ill may come thee near,
My bonie dearie.

Fair and lovely as thou art, *ert*
Thou hast stown[9] my very heart; *hert*
dee I can die — but canna part, *pairt*
My bonie dearie.

[1] drive the ewes to the knolls [2] brook runs [3] thrush's
[4] gathering the sheep [5] go [6] go [7] ghost nor spectre
[8] nothing [9] stolen

8. Ca' the yowes to the knowes

Tune:— Ca' the Yowes. S.M.M. 1790, No. 264.

9. Is there for honest poverty

"A great critic (Aikin) on songs says that Love and Wine are the exclusive themes for song-writing. This is on neither subject and consequently is no song — but will be allowed, I think, to be two or three pretty good prose thoughts inverted into rhyme . . . I do not give you the foregoing song for your book, but merely by way of *vive la bagatelle:* for the piece is not really poetry."

(Letter to Thomson, 1 Jan., 1795)

	Is there for honest poverty	*oanist poavurtay*
	That hings[1] his head, an' a' that?	*heed*
coourd	The coward slave, we pass him by—	
dawr, pair	We dare be poor for a' that![2]	
	For a' that, an' a' that,	
teilz	Our toils obscure, an' a' that,	
	The rank is but the guinea's stamp,	*geeniz*
	The man's the gowd[3] for a' that.	
	What though on hamely[4] fare we dine,	
weer hoadun	Wear hodden grey, [5] an' a' that.	
fillz, sulks	Gie fools their silks, and knaves their wine—	
	A man's a man for a' that.	
	For a' that, an' a' that,	
	Their tinsel show, an' a' that,	
oanist	The honest man, tho' e'er sae poor,	*pair*
keeng	Is king o' men for a' that.	
yoan	Ye see yon birkie[6] ca'd a lord,	*loard*
	Wha struts, an' stares, an' a' that?	
hunurz	Tho' hundreds worship at his word,	
kiff	He's but a cuif[7] for a' that.	
	For a' that, an' a' that,	
ribun, stawr	His ribband, star, an' a' that,	
	The man o' independent mind,	*mein*
luks	He looks and laughs at a' that.	*lawchs*
	A prince can mak a belted knight,	*nicht*
markis	A marquis, duke, an' a' that!	
oanist	But an honest man's aboon[8] his micht—	*ubin, micht*
	Guid faith, he mauna fa' that![9]	
	For a' that, an' a' that,	
	Their dignities, an' a' that,	
	The pith o' sense, an' pride o' worth	
heechur	Are higher rank than a' that.	
	Then let us pray that come it may	
	As come it will, for a' that—	
	That sense and worth o'er a' the earth	*owr*
	Shall bear the gree[10] an' a' that;	
	For a' that, an' a' that,	
	It's comin' yet for a' that,	
	That man to man the world o'er	
britherz	Shall brothers be for a' that.	

[1]hangs [2]all that [3]gold [4]homely [5]coarse home made woollen cloth
[6]fellow [7]fool [8]above [9]he can't be allowed to claim that
[10]take first place

9. Is there for honest poverty

Tune:— For a' that.

S.M.M. 1790, 290.

10. My love, she's but a lassie yet

The title and the last half stanza of the song are old; the rest was composed by Burns.

— (Stenhouse)

My love, she's but a lassie yet,
My love, she's but a lassie yet!
stawn We'll let her stand a year or twa,
hawf She'll no be half sae saucy yet!

I rue the day I sought her, O, *socht*
I rue the day I sought her, O!
Wha gets her needna say he's woo'd,
But he may say he's bought her, O! *bocht*

Come draw a drap[1] o' the best o't yet,
Come draw a drap o' the best o't yet!
pleezhur Gae seek for pleasure whare ye will, *wull*
But here I never missed it yet.

We're a' dry wi' drinkin' o't,
We're a' dry wi' drinkin' o't!
meenister The minister kiss't the fiddler's wife—
He could na preach for thinkin' o't!

[1] drop

10. My love, she's but a lassie yet

Tune:— My love, she's but a lassie yet. S.M.M. 1790, 225.

11. Lassie wi' the lint-white locks

"This piece has at least the merit of being a regular pastoral; the vernal morn, the summer noon, the autumnal evening and the winter night are regularly rounded."
(Letter to Thomson, Nov., 1794)

Chorus

Lassie wi' the lint-white[1] locks — *loaks*
boanay — Bonie lassie, artless lassie
Wilt thou wi' me tent[2] the flocks— — *floaks*
Wilt thou be my dearie, O?

noo Naitur — Now Nature cleeds[3] the flowery lea, — *flooray*
And a' is young and sweet like thee,
O, wilt thou share its joys wi' me,
And say thou'lt be my dearie, O?

The primrose bank, the wimpling[4] burn,
The cuckoo on the milk-white thorn
The wanton lambs at early morn
Shall welcome thee, my dearie, O.

And when the welcome simmer[5] shower — *shoor*
Has cheer'd ilk[6] drooping little flower — *floor*
We'll to the breathing woodbine-bower
At sultry noon, my dearie, O.

lichts — When Cynthia[7] lights, wi' silver ray
The weary shearer's[8] hameward way;
Thro' yellow waving fields we'll stray,
And talk o' love, my dearie, O.

And when the howling wintry blast — *blest*
Disturbs my lassie's midnight rest,
Enclasped to my faithfu' brest,
I'll comfort thee, my dearie, O.

[1] flaxen [2] tend, watch [3] clothes [4] meandering [5] summer
[6] each [7] the moon [8] reaper's

11. Lassie wi' the lint-white locks

Tune:— Rothiemurche's rant.

Scotish Airs, 1801, 121.

12. My hearts in the highlands

"The first half stanza of this song is old; the rest is mine."
(R. B. in *Interleaved Museum)*

My heart's in the Highlands, my heart is not here,
My heart's in the Highlands a-chasing the deer,
A-chasing the wild deer, and following the roe—
My heart's in the Highlands, wherever I go.

Farewell to the Highlands, farewell to the North—
The birthplace of valour, the country of worth:
Wherever I wander, wherever I rove,
The hills of the Highlands for ever I love.

Farewell to the mountains high cover'd with snow,
Farewell to the straths and green valleys below,
Farewell to the forests and wild-hanging woods,
Farewell to the torrents and loud-pouring floods!

12. My heart's in the Highlands

Tune:— Crochallan.

R. A. Smith's Scottish Minstrel IV.4, 1820-1824.

13. A red, red rose

This song was published in the *Scots Musical Museum,* 1796, No. 402, to the tune *Major Graham,* but is now invariably sung to a modern version of *Low down in the broom.*

My luve is like a red, red rose, *rid*
That's newly sprung in June. *Jin*
My luve is like the melodie, *mailoday*
That's sweetly play'd in tune. *tin*
As fair art thou, my bonie lass, *boanay*
sae So deep in luve am I,
And I will luve thee still, my dear,
Till a' the seas gang dry.

Till a' the seas gang dry, my dear,
roaks And the rocks melt wi' the sun!
And I will luve thee still, my dear,
While the sands o' life shall run.
And fare thee weel, my only luve,
And fare thee weel a while!
And I will come again my luve,
Tho' it were ten thousand mile! *thoozun*

13. A red, red rose

Tune:— Low down in the broom.

R. A. Smith's Scottish Minstrel III. 81, 1820-1824.

14. O, wert thou in the cauld blast

Written during his last illness in honour of Jessie Lewars, after she had played *The Wren,* or *Lenox love to Blantyre,* to him on the harpsichord until he was familiar with the air

(Chambers, IV, 267)

	O, wert thou in the cauld[1] blast	*cawl*
	On yonder lea, on yonder lea,	*yoandur*
pleiday	My plaidie to the angry airt[2]	
	I'd shelter thee, I'd shelter thee.	
misfoartinz	Or did Misfortune's bitter storms	*stoarmz*
uroon	Around thee blaw,[3] around thee blaw,	
biel	Thy bield[4] should be my bosom,	
	To share it a', to share it a'.	
	Or were I in the wildest waste,	
	Sae[5] black and bare, sae black and bare,	
daizurt	The desert were a paradise,	
	If thou wert there, if thou wert there.	
	Or were I monarch of the globe,	
	Wi' thee to reign, wi' thee to reign,	
brichtest	The brightest jewel in my crown	*croon*
	Wad[6] be my queen, wad be my queen.	

[1] cold [2] direction of the wind [3] blow [4] shelter [5] so [6] would

14. O, wert thou in the cauld blast

Tune:— Lenox love to Blantyre. S.M.M. 1796, 483.

15. O, whistle an' I'll come to ye, my lad

The heroine of this song was Jean Lorimer.
(Letter to Thomson, 3 August, 1795)

Chorus

O, whistle, an' I'll come to ye, my lad! *tae*
O, whistle, an' I'll come to ye, my lad!
faithur, mithur Through father an' mother an' a' should gae mad,
O, whistle an' I'll come to ye, my lad!

But warily tent[1] when ye come to court me *coort*
And come nae unless the back-yett be a-jee;[2]
Syne up the back-style,[3] and let naebody see,
And come as ye were na comin to me,
And come as ye were na comin to me.

merkit At kirk, or at market, whene'er ye meet me,
Gang by me as tho' that ye car'd na a flie;[4] *flee*
But steal me a blink[5] o' your bonie black e'e,[6] *boanay*
Yet look as ye were na lookin at me,
Yet look as ye were na lookin at me.

ei Ay vow and protest that ye care na for me,
lichtlay And whiles ye may lightly[7] my beauty a wee;
But court na anither, tho' jokin' ye be,
For fear that she wile your fancy frae me,
For fear that she wile your fancy frae me.

[1] heed [2] backgate be ajar [3] passage [4] didn't care a bit
[5] glance [6] eye [7] disparage, make light of

15. O, whistle, an' I'll come to ye, my lad

Tune:— Whistle an' I'll come to ye, my lad. S.M.M. 1788, 106.

16. There was a lad was born in Kyle

"The date of my Bardship's vital existence."
(Burns's note on MS of second stanza)

The song was written to the tune *Dainty Davie.* John Templeton, the tenor vocalist, brought it to public notice, but he selected the tune, *O, an ye were dead, Guidman,* to which it is almost always sung.

lawd	There was a lad was born in Kyle,	*boarn*
hwitna	But whatna day o' whatna style,[1]	
doot	I doubt it's hardly worth the while	*hawrlay*
	To be sae nice[2] wi' Robin.	

Chorus

Roabin	Robin was a rovin' boy,	*roavin*
	Rantin,[3] rovin, rantin, rovin,	
	Robin was a rovin boy,	
	Rantin, rovin Robin!	

hinmust	Our monarch's hindmost[4] year but ane	*yin*
twintie	Was five-and-twenty days begun,	
than	'Twas then a blast o' Janwar'[5] win'	*Jenwur*
	Blew hansel[6] in on Robin.	

goasup	The gossip keekit in his loof	*liff*
leevz	Quo scho[8]:—"Wha lives will see the proof,	*priff*
wawlay	This waly[9] boy will be nae coof:[10]	*kiff*
	I think we'll ca' him Robin.	*caw*

misfoartinz	"He'll hae misfortunes great an' sma,'	
ei hert	But ay[11] a heart aboon them a',	*ubin*
craidit	He'll be a credit till us a':	
	We'll a' be proud o' Robin!	*prood*

shair	"But sure as three times three mak nine,	
	I see by ilka[12] score and line,	
	This chap will dearly like our kin',[13]	*oor kein*
sae	So leeze me on thee[14] Robin!"	

[1]which style (old or new) [2]particular [3]high-spirited [4]last
[5]January, [6]a gift for luck [7]peeped into his palm [8]quoth she
[9]fine [10]fool [11]always [12]each [13](the lassies)
[14]my love to you

16. There was a lad was born in Kyle

Tune:— O, an ye were dead, Guidman. Cal. Pocket Companion 1752, IV p. 24.

17. The banks o' Doon

(THIRD VERSION)

An Ayrshire legend says the heroine of this song was Peggy Kennedy of Daljarrock
(Allan Cunningham)

Ye banks and braes[1] o' bonie Doon, — *boanay Din*
How can ye bloom sae fresh and fair?
hoo — How can ye chant, ye little birds,
And I sae weary fu' o' care!
brek, hert — Thou'll break my heart, thou warbling bird,
That wantons thro' the flowering thorn! — *floorin thoarn*
Thou minds[2] me o' departed joys, — *dipairtit*
Departed never to return.

Aft hae[3] I rov'd by bonie Doon — *boanay Din*
To see the rose and woodbine[4] twine, — *widbein*
And ilka[5] bird sang o' its luve,
foandlay — And fondly sae did I o' mine.
lichtsome hert — Wi' lightsome heart I pu'd[6] a rose,
Fu' sweet upon its thorny tree! — *thoarnay*
And my fause[7] luver staw[8] my rose —
But ah! he left the thorn wi' me. — *thoarn*

[1] slopes [2] remindest [3] often have [4] honeysuckle [5] every
[6] pulled [6] false [8] stole

17. The banks o' Doon

Tune:— The Caledonian Hunt's delight

S.M.M. 1792, No. 374.

18. The birks of Aberfeldy

"I composed these stanzas standing under the Falls of Aberfeldy at or near Moness."
(R. B. in *Interleaved Museum)*

Chorus

boanay Bonie lassie, will ye go,
Will ye go, will ye go?
Bonie lassie, will ye go
tae To the birks[1] of Aberfeldy?

Now Simmer[2] blinks[3] on flow'ry braes, *flooray*
owr And o'er the crystal streamlets plays;
Come, let us spend the lightsome[4] days *lichtsum*
In the birks of Aberfeldy.

The little birdies blythely sing,
While o'er their heads the hazels hing,[5]
lichtlay Or lightly flit on wanton wing
In the birks of Aberfeldy.

The braes[6] ascend like lofty wa's, *wawz*
The foaming stream, deep-roaring, fa's *fawz*
O'erhung wi' fragrant-spreading shaws[7]
The birks of Aberfeldy.

The hoary cliffs are crown'd wi flowers, *crooned, floorz*
owr White o'er the linns[8] the burnie pours, *poorz*
And, rising, weets[9] wi' misty showers *shoorz*
The birks of Aberfeldy.

Foartinz Let Fortune's gifts at random flee,
They ne'er shall draw a wish frae me;
Supremely blest wi' love and thee
In the birks of Aberfeldy.

[1] birches [2] summer [3] shines [4] merry [5] hang [6] hillsides
[7] woods [9] waterfalls [9] wets

18. The Birks of Aberfeldy

Tune:—Birks of Abergeldie.

S.M.M. 1788, No. 113.

19. This is no my ain lassie

"*This is no my ain house* puzzles me a good deal; in fact I think to change the old rhythm of the first, or chorus part of the tune, will have a good effect. I would have it something like the gallop of the following."

(Letter to Thomson, 3 July, 1795)

Chorus

This is no my ain[1] lassie,
Fair tho' the lassie be;
Weel ken[2] I my ain lassie,
Kind love is in her e'e.

foarm I see a form, I see a face,
Ye weel may wi' the fairest place;
It wants to me the witching grace,
The kind love that's in her e'e.

boanay She's bonie, blooming, straight, and tall, *strawcht*
And lang has had my heart in thrall; *hert*
ei, chairmz And ay it charms my very saul,[3]
The kind of love that's in her e'e.

A thief sae pawkie[4] is my Jean,
To steal a blink[5] by a' unseen!
licht But gleg[6] as light are lovers' een,
When kind love is in the e'e.

It may escape the courtly sparks,
It may escape the learned clerks;
But weel the watching lover marks
The kind love that's in her e'e.

[1] own [2] know [3] soul [4] sly [5] glance [6] quick

19. This is no my ain lassie

Tune:— This is no my ain house. Scotish Airs, 1799, 56.

20. Auld lang syne

Burns sent to George Thomson a copy of this song as it was later published in the *Scots Musical Museum* in 1796. Thomson apparently consulted Burns about the tune and the poet referred to the *Museum* air as mediocre.

(Letter to Thomson, Sept., 1793)

This popular melody is a variant of *O can ye labor lea,* to which Burns wrote *I fee'd a man at Martinmas.*

(S.M.M., 1792, No. 394)

awl akwantuns	Should auld acquaintance be forgot,	*furgoat*
	And never brought to mind?	*broacht, mein*
	Should auld acquaintance be forgot,	
	And days o' lang syne![1]	*sein*
	For Auld lang syne, my dear,	
	For auld lang syne,	
	We'll tak a cup o' kindness yet	*keinnus*
	For auld lang syne!	
shairlay	And surely ye'll be[2] your pint-stowp,	*stowp*
	And surely I'll be mine,	
	And we'll tak a cup o' kindness yet	
	For auld lang syne!	
	We twa hae run about the braes,[3]	
pood	And pou'd the gowans[4] fine,	
wawnurt munnay	But we've wander'd mony[5] a weary foot	*fit*
	Sin[6] auld lang syne.	
	We twa he paidl'd[7] in the burn	
	Frae morning sun till dine,[8]	
	But seas between us braid[9] hae roar'd	
	Sin auld lang syne.	
hawn	And there's a hand, my trusty fiere,[11]	*feer*
geez	And gie's[11] a hand o' thine,	
	And we'll tak a right gude-willie waught[12]	*richt gid-wullie wawcht*
	For auld lang syne!	

[1] days of long ago [2] pay for [3] hillsides [4] pulled the daisies
[5] many [6] since [7] waded [8] dinner-time [9] broad [10] chum
[11] give us [12] friendly draught

20. # Auld lang syne

Tune:— Auld Lang Syne.

Scotish Airs, 1799, 68.

Printed by Sunprint, 36 Tay Street, Perth and 40 Craigs, Stirling